COIN INVENTORY

LOG BOOK

Name: _______________

Phone: _______________

Coin Inventory Log

Date ____________________   Page no. ____________

Item	Description	Qty	Mint	Grade	Source	Purchase Date	Price

Coin Inventory Log

Date ____________________ Page no. ____________________

Item	Description	Qty	Mint	Grade	Source	Purchase Date	Price

Coin Inventory Log

Date: _______________   Page no. _______________

Item	Description	Qty	Mint	Grade	Source	Purchase Date	Price

Coin Inventory Log

Date ___________ **Page no.** ___________

Item	Description	Qty	Mint	Grade	Source	Purchase Date	Price

Coin Inventory Log

Date ______________________ Page no. ______________________

Item	Description	Qty	Mint	Grade	Source	Purchase Date	Price

Coin Inventory Log

Date ___________   Page no. ___________

Item	Description	Qty	Mint	Grade	Source	Purchase Date	Price

Coin Inventory Log

Date _______________   Page no. _______

Item	Description	Qty	Mint	Grade	Source	Purchase Date	Price

Coin Inventory Log

Date ___________________ Page no. ___________________

Item	Description	Qty	Mint	Grade	Source	Purchase Date	Price

Coin Inventory Log

Date **_______________** Page no. **_______________**

Item	Description	Qty	Mint	Grade	Source	Purchase Date	Price

Coin Inventory Log

Date ______________________   **Page no.** ______________________

Item	Description	Qty	Mint	Grade	Source	Purchase Date	Price

Coin Inventory Log

Date ___________   **Page no.** ___________

Item	Description	Qty	Mint	Grade	Source	Purchase Date	Price

Coin Inventory Log

Date _______________ **Page no.** _______________

Item	Description	Qty	Mint	Grade	Source	Purchase Date	Price

Coin Inventory Log

Date _______________ Page no. _______________

Item	Description	Qty	Mint	Grade	Source	Purchase Date	Price

Coin Inventory Log

Date ___________ Page no. ___________

Item	Description	Qty	Mint	Grade	Source	Purchase Date	Price

Coin Inventory Log

Date ___________________ Page no. ___________________

Item	Description	Qty	Mint	Grade	Source	Purchase Date	Price

Coin Inventory Log

Date _______________   Page no. _______________

Item	Description	Qty	Mint	Grade	Source	Purchase Date	Price

Coin Inventory Log

Date ___________________ Page no. ___________________

Item	Description	Qty	Mint	Grade	Source	Purchase Date	Price

Coin Inventory Log

Date   Page no.

Item	Description	Qty	Mint	Grade	Source	Purchase Date	Price

Coin Inventory Log

Date ______________________   Page no. ______________________

Item	Description	Qty	Mint	Grade	Source	Purchase Date	Price

Coin Inventory Log

Date ___________________   **Page no.** ___________

Item	Description	Qty	Mint	Grade	Source	Purchase Date	Price

Coin Inventory Log

Date _______________ Page no. _______________

Item	Description	Qty	Mint	Grade	Source	Purchase Date	Price

Coin Inventory Log

Date _______________   Page no. _______________

Item	Description	Qty	Mint	Grade	Source	Purchase Date	Price

Coin Inventory Log

Date ___________________ Page no. ___________________

Item	Description	Qty	Mint	Grade	Source	Purchase Date	Price

Coin Inventory Log

Date ____________________ Page no. ____________

Item	Description	Qty	Mint	Grade	Source	Purchase Date	Price

Coin Inventory Log

Date ______________________   **Page no.** ______________________

Item	Description	Qty	Mint	Grade	Source	Purchase Date	Price

Coin Inventory Log

Date ___________________   Page no. ___________

Item	Description	Qty	Mint	Grade	Source	Purchase Date	Price

Coin Inventory Log

Date ______________________   Page no. ______________________

Item	Description	Qty	Mint	Grade	Source	Purchase Date	Price

Coin Inventory Log

Date ____________________   Page no. ____________

Item	Description	Qty	Mint	Grade	Source	Purchase Date	Price

Coin Inventory Log

Date ____________________   Page no. ____________

Item	Description	Qty	Mint	Grade	Source	Purchase Date	Price

Coin Inventory Log

Date ____________________   Page no. ____________________

Item	Description	Qty	Mint	Grade	Source	Purchase Date	Price

Coin Inventory Log

Date: _______________   Page no. _______________

Item	Description	Qty	Mint	Grade	Source	Purchase Date	Price

Coin Inventory Log

Date _______________ **Page no.** _______________

Item	Description	Qty	Mint	Grade	Source	Purchase Date	Price

Coin Inventory Log

Date _______________   Page no. _______________

Item	Description	Qty	Mint	Grade	Source	Purchase Date	Price

Coin Inventory Log

Date _______________   Page no. _______________

Item	Description	Qty	Mint	Grade	Source	Purchase Date	Price

Coin Inventory Log

Date _______________   Page no. _______________

Item	Description	Qty	Mint	Grade	Source	Purchase Date	Price

Coin Inventory Log

Date ______________   Page no. ______________

Item	Description	Qty	Mint	Grade	Source	Purchase Date	Price

Coin Inventory Log

Date ______________________   Page no. ______________________

Item	Description	Qty	Mint	Grade	Source	Purchase Date	Price

Coin Inventory Log

Date ______________   Page no. ______________

Item	Description	Qty	Mint	Grade	Source	Purchase Date	Price

Coin Inventory Log

Date _______________   Page no. _______________

Item	Description	Qty	Mint	Grade	Source	Purchase Date	Price

Coin Inventory Log

Date _______________   Page no. _______________

Item	Description	Qty	Mint	Grade	Source	Purchase Date	Price

Coin Inventory Log

Date ____________________   Page no. ____________________

Item	Description	Qty	Mint	Grade	Source	Purchase Date	Price

Coin Inventory Log

Date

Page no.

Item	Description	Qty	Mint	Grade	Source	Purchase Date	Price

Coin Inventory Log

Date ________________   Page no. ________________

Item	Description	Qty	Mint	Grade	Source	Purchase Date	Price

Coin Inventory Log

Date ___________   **Page no.** ___________

Item	Description	Qty	Mint	Grade	Source	Purchase Date	Price

Coin Inventory Log

Date ____________________   Page no. ____________________

Item	Description	Qty	Mint	Grade	Source	Purchase Date	Price

Coin Inventory Log

Date ______________________   **Page no.** ______________________

Item	Description	Qty	Mint	Grade	Source	Purchase Date	Price

Coin Inventory Log

Date ___________________ **Page no.** ___________

Item	Description	Qty	Mint	Grade	Source	Purchase Date	Price

Coin Inventory Log

Date ____________________ **Page no.** ____________________

Item	Description	Qty	Mint	Grade	Source	Purchase Date	Price

Coin Inventory Log

Date **________**   Page no. **_______**

Item	Description	Qty	Mint	Grade	Source	Purchase Date	Price

Coin Inventory Log

Date ____________________   Page no. ____________________

Item	Description	Qty	Mint	Grade	Source	Purchase Date	Price

Coin Inventory Log

Date _______________   Page no. _______________

Item	Description	Qty	Mint	Grade	Source	Purchase Date	Price

Coin Inventory Log

Date _______________ Page no. _______________

Item	Description	Qty	Mint	Grade	Source	Purchase Date	Price

Coin Inventory Log

Date   Page no.

Item	Description	Qty	Mint	Grade	Source	Purchase Date	Price

Coin Inventory Log

Date ____________________   **Page no.** ____________________

Item	Description	Qty	Mint	Grade	Source	Purchase Date	Price

Coin Inventory Log

Date ____________________ Page no. ____________________

Item	Description	Qty	Mint	Grade	Source	Purchase Date	Price

Coin Inventory Log

Date _______________   Page no. _______________

Item	Description	Qty	Mint	Grade	Source	Purchase Date	Price

Coin Inventory Log

Date ______________________   **Page no.** ______________

Item	Description	Qty	Mint	Grade	Source	Purchase Date	Price

Coin Inventory Log

Date ___________________   Page no. ___________________

Item	Description	Qty	Mint	Grade	Source	Purchase Date	Price

Coin Inventory Log

Date _______________ Page no. _______________

Item	Description	Qty	Mint	Grade	Source	Purchase Date	Price

Coin Inventory Log

Date   Page no.

Item	Description	Qty	Mint	Grade	Source	Purchase Date	Price

Coin Inventory Log

Date ____________________   Page no. __________

Item	Description	Qty	Mint	Grade	Source	Purchase Date	Price

Coin Inventory Log

Date ___________ Page no. ___________

Item	Description	Qty	Mint	Grade	Source	Purchase Date	Price

Coin Inventory Log

Date _______________ Page no. _______________

Item	Description	Qty	Mint	Grade	Source	Purchase Date	Price

Coin Inventory Log

Date __________________   **Page no.** __________________

Item	Description	Qty	Mint	Grade	Source	Purchase Date	Price

Coin Inventory Log

Date _______________________ **Page no.** _______________________

Item	Description	Qty	Mint	Grade	Source	Purchase Date	Price

Coin Inventory Log

Date ____________________   Page no. ____________

Item	Description	Qty	Mint	Grade	Source	Purchase Date	Price

Coin Inventory Log

Date ___________ Page no. ___________

Item	Description	Qty	Mint	Grade	Source	Purchase Date	Price

Coin Inventory Log

Date ___________________   Page no. ___________________

Item	Description	Qty	Mint	Grade	Source	Purchase Date	Price

Coin Inventory Log

Date _________________ Page no. _________

Item	Description	Qty	Mint	Grade	Source	Purchase Date	Price

Coin Inventory Log

Date __________ Page no. __________

Item	Description	Qty	Mint	Grade	Source	Purchase Date	Price

Coin Inventory Log

Date __________________   Page no. __________________

Item	Description	Qty	Mint	Grade	Source	Purchase Date	Price

Coin Inventory Log

Date ______________________   Page no. ______________________

Item	Description	Qty	Mint	Grade	Source	Purchase Date	Price

Coin Inventory Log

Date ____________________   Page no. ____________________

Item	Description	Qty	Mint	Grade	Source	Purchase Date	Price

Coin Inventory Log

Date ____________________   Page no. ____________________

Item	Description	Qty	Mint	Grade	Source	Purchase Date	Price

Coin Inventory Log

Date _______________________ Page no. _______________

Item	Description	Qty	Mint	Grade	Source	Purchase Date	Price

Coin Inventory Log

Date __________________   Page no. __________________

Item	Description	Qty	Mint	Grade	Source	Purchase Date	Price

Coin Inventory Log

Date ____________________   **Page no.** ____________________

Item	Description	Qty	Mint	Grade	Source	Purchase Date	Price

Coin Inventory Log

Date _______________   Page no. _______________

Item	Description	Qty	Mint	Grade	Source	Purchase Date	Price

Coin Inventory Log

Date ___________________   Page no. ___________________

Item	Description	Qty	Mint	Grade	Source	Purchase Date	Price

Coin Inventory Log

Date _______________ Page no. _______

Item	Description	Qty	Mint	Grade	Source	Purchase Date	Price

Coin Inventory Log

Date ___________________   Page no. ___________________

Item	Description	Qty	Mint	Grade	Source	Purchase Date	Price

Coin Inventory Log

Date _______________   Page no. _______________

Item	Description	Qty	Mint	Grade	Source	Purchase Date	Price

Coin Inventory Log

Date ____________________ Page no. ____________

Item	Description	Qty	Mint	Grade	Source	Purchase Date	Price

Coin Inventory Log

Date   Page no.

Item	Description	Qty	Mint	Grade	Source	Purchase Date	Price

Coin Inventory Log

Date _______________   Page no. _______________

Item	Description	Qty	Mint	Grade	Source	Purchase Date	Price

Coin Inventory Log

Date ____________________   **Page no.** ____________________

Item	Description	Qty	Mint	Grade	Source	Purchase Date	Price

Coin Inventory Log

Date _______________   Page no. _______________

Item	Description	Qty	Mint	Grade	Source	Purchase Date	Price

Coin Inventory Log

Date   **Page no.**

Item	Description	Qty	Mint	Grade	Source	Purchase Date	Price

Coin Inventory Log

Date ______________________   Page no. ______________

Item	Description	Qty	Mint	Grade	Source	Purchase Date	Price

Coin Inventory Log

Date ____________________ **Page no.** ____________________

Item	Description	Qty	Mint	Grade	Source	Purchase Date	Price

Coin Inventory Log

Date **___________**   Page no. **___________**

Item	Description	Qty	Mint	Grade	Source	Purchase Date	Price

Coin Inventory Log

Date _______________ **Page no.** _______________

Item	Description	Qty	Mint	Grade	Source	Purchase Date	Price

Coin Inventory Log

Date _______________   Page no. _______________

Item	Description	Qty	Mint	Grade	Source	Purchase Date	Price

Coin Inventory Log

Date

Page no.

Item	Description	Qty	Mint	Grade	Source	Purchase Date	Price

Coin Inventory Log

Date _______________   Page no. _______________

Item	Description	Qty	Mint	Grade	Source	Purchase Date	Price

Coin Inventory Log

Date ____________________   Page no. ____________

Item	Description	Qty	Mint	Grade	Source	Purchase Date	Price

Coin Inventory Log

Date ____________________ Page no. __________

Item	Description	Qty	Mint	Grade	Source	Purchase Date	Price

Coin Inventory Log

Date ___________   Page no. ___________

Item	Description	Qty	Mint	Grade	Source	Purchase Date	Price

Coin Inventory Log

Date __________________   Page no. __________________

Item	Description	Qty	Mint	Grade	Source	Purchase Date	Price

Coin Inventory Log

Date ___________ **Page no.** ___________

Item	Description	Qty	Mint	Grade	Source	Purchase Date	Price

Coin Inventory Log

Date _______________   Page no. _______________

Item	Description	Qty	Mint	Grade	Source	Purchase Date	Price

Coin Inventory Log

Date _______________   Page no. _______________

Item	Description	Qty	Mint	Grade	Source	Purchase Date	Price

Coin Inventory Log

Date

Page no.

Item	Description	Qty	Mint	Grade	Source	Purchase Date	Price

Coin Inventory Log

Date ___________________ Page no. __________

Item	Description	Qty	Mint	Grade	Source	Purchase Date	Price

Coin Inventory Log

Date ____________   Page no. ____________

Item	Description	Qty	Mint	Grade	Source	Purchase Date	Price

Coin Inventory Log

Date ___________________ **Page no.** ___________________

Item	Description	Qty	Mint	Grade	Source	Purchase Date	Price

Coin Inventory Log

Date _______________   **Page no.** _______________

Item	Description	Qty	Mint	Grade	Source	Purchase Date	Price

Coin Inventory Log

Date _______________   Page no. _______________

Item	Description	Qty	Mint	Grade	Source	Purchase Date	Price

Coin Inventory Log

Date _______________ Page no. _______________

Item	Description	Qty	Mint	Grade	Source	Purchase Date	Price

Coin Inventory Log

Date _______________   Page no. _______________

Item	Description	Qty	Mint	Grade	Source	Purchase Date	Price

Coin Inventory Log

Date ___________________ Page no. ___________

Item	Description	Qty	Mint	Grade	Source	Purchase Date	Price

Coin Inventory Log

Date ___________________ **Page no.** ___________

Item	Description	Qty	Mint	Grade	Source	Purchase Date	Price

Coin Inventory Log

Date ____________________   Page no. ____________

Item	Description	Qty	Mint	Grade	Source	Purchase Date	Price

Coin Inventory Log

Date ____________________   Page no. ____________________

Item	Description	Qty	Mint	Grade	Source	Purchase Date	Price

Coin Inventory Log

Date ___________________   Page no. ___________________

Item	Description	Qty	Mint	Grade	Source	Purchase Date	Price

Coin Inventory Log

Date ____________________   Page no. __________

Item	Description	Qty	Mint	Grade	Source	Purchase Date	Price

Coin Inventory Log

Date ____________________   Page no. __________

Item	Description	Qty	Mint	Grade	Source	Purchase Date	Price

Coin Inventory Log

Date ____________________ Page no. ____________

Item	Description	Qty	Mint	Grade	Source	Purchase Date	Price